Steps Toward Belonging

For Cat,

Thanks for your support
for the launch of this book!

Much love,
Sandy

Steps Toward Belonging

A 31-Day Journey with God

Sandy Salisbury

Cover design by Graeme Salisbury.

Edited by Ashley Casteel.

To contact the author, visit www.sandysalisbury.com, or email sjsalisbury@outlook.com.

Contents

Foreword

"Church would be fine if it wasn't for the people." It's a phrase as old as the day is long, and yet, like many such maxims, we know that it endures because it speaks to what most of us have learned the hard way. But to be a follower of Jesus is not only an invitation to dependency on him; it's also an allegiance that asks us to enter into another realm of kinships, new ways of relating to people within and without the community of faith.

Often these relationships are complicated. We find it has always been this way as we survey the letters written by apostles to the earliest churches. We read about the law-keepers who clashed with the grace lobby in Galatia, the factions that formed because of conflicting loyalties to different leaders in Corinth, and the freeloaders who took others for granted in Thessalonica. In *Steps Toward Belonging*, Sandy Salisbury takes us on a journey which includes visits to some of these developing Christian communities, and others besides, while also reaching back into the stories and wisdom literature of the Old Testament. Invariably, the conclusions she draws are profound yet disarming, throwing up a mirror against defensive or self-justifying attitudes that we will all recognize in ourselves.

These reflections brim with memorable imagery you can carry with you through the day or the week. Continue reading, and you will discover things you didn't realize about drainage in vineyards, burrowing elephants, string theory, and tea strainers. The illustrations open up important and perceptive insights about journeying in community with others.

These observations offer practical encouragement to open our eyes, ears, and hearts not only to God but also to the other people with whom we live, work, play, and worship. We are prompted to develop a greater empathy for others and to seek a higher level of self-awareness. For those, like myself, who have had the privilege of worshiping and leading alongside Sandy for many years, part of the appeal and credibility of these studies will come from hearing the same voice with which she has spoken into situations where clarity and wisdom were urgently needed. If you are discovering her work for the first time, prepare to lower your defenses as you encounter a fresh and honest voice that will enable you to be stretched and stimulated in your understanding of God and others.

Among the many helpful pieces of advice found in *Steps Toward Belonging* is one which asks us to "embrace the irritations that come with being part of a community. If handled well, they can become seeds of beauty." Embrace also, with open arms, the wisdom that is found here. If you do, you will discover it to be a blessing not only for yourself but also for those around you.

Trevor Neill
lead pastor of Selsdon Baptist Church

Introduction

"If we have no peace, it is because we have forgotten that we belong to each other."

MOTHER TERESA

Our society is fractured. I'm fractured. God created us to connect in relationships—with Him and with each other. All of us want to "belong"; it's part of our DNA. But so many of us feel at times—or even all the time—that we don't belong. We're on the outside, on the fringes, and don't know how to join in.

Respected moral thinker, philosopher, and scholar Rabbi Lord Jonathan Sacks says, "In thinking about religion and society in the twenty-first century, we should broaden the conversation about faith from doctrinal debates to the larger question of how it might inspire us to strengthen the bonds of belonging that redeem us from our solitude, helping us to construct together a gracious and generous social order." [i]

God's kingdom represents the kind of community we all want—where everyone is accepted just as they are, where people communicate transparently, where there is plenty for all and everyone shares, where people respect each other and care for each other freely. We already belong to communities, whether we choose them or not—our families, our neighborhoods, our workplaces. They often fail to live up to the Kingdom ideal. The challenge is to accept the communities we've been placed in and do our bit to transform them.

Dr. Neil T. Anderson, evangelist and author of *Steps to Freedom in Christ*, says, "Aloneness can lead to loneliness. God's preventative for loneliness is intimacy—meaningful, open, sharing relationships with one another. In Christ we have the capacity for the fulfilling sense of belonging which comes from intimate fellowship with God and with other believers."

Jesus modeled belonging, and the Bible is the story of God inviting us to belong to His family. Let's go on a journey together and learn how to join in. It is the way to fulfil our purpose, and to be who we are meant to be.

Sandy Salisbury

Steps Toward Belonging: Studies

"The confidence that God is mindful of the individual is of tremendous value in dealing with the disease of fear, for it gives us a sense of worth, of belonging, and of at-homeness in the universe."

MARTIN LUTHER

A: Starting Out

1. The Invitation – Matthew 11:25-30

God doesn't *need* us to do anything for Him—He is God! Neither does He *ask* for our help, as if we could assist Him in any way.

Rather, God *invites* us to join Him in Kingdom work.

If we don't recognize this invitation when it comes, He patiently invites us again. If we don't respond to the invitation, He waits until we are ready to respond. Even if we actively reject His invitation, He doesn't take offense in the way we might if our friends were to reject an invitation from us. He is persistent, but not insistent.

We are the ones who put up barriers to accepting His invitation. We may miss an invitation because our inbox is too full. The invitation might get buried under paperwork. We may have noticed the invitation but forgot to put it on our calendar. We may not want to go to the event because we are uncomfortable around others who are going. We may not feel we can spare the time. Or we may think that accepting the invitation will entail an expense we cannot afford (a new outfit, an appropriate gift, travel costs, etc.).

[Jesus said,] "Come to me, all you who are weary and burdened, and I will give you rest. Take my yoke upon you and learn from me, for I am gentle and humble in heart, and you will find rest for your souls. For my yoke is easy and my burden is light."

MATTHEW 11:28–30

If we listen to Jesus's invitation carefully, we will realize that it needs to go to the top of the pile. We will want to make time for His calling, because it is by far the best event on the calendar. Responding may mean mixing with people we wouldn't otherwise have chosen, but when we do, we will be amazed at the richness of the experience. And accepting His invitation is not nearly as expensive as refusing it, in terms of life stress and anxiety.

We may need help in knocking down the barriers to the ongoing, life-changing, marvelous invitation God gives. God's invitation enables us to leave our anxieties behind. Let's encourage each other to accept what God is prompting us to do today.

- What is God prompting you to do today? Let go of the anxiety and get on with it!
- Find a way this week to encourage one person to come closer to Jesus.

God's invitation to us is always there.

2. Living with God on His Holy Hill – Psalm 15

Who may live on your holy mountain?

The one whose walk is blameless, who does what is righteous, who speaks the truth from their heart; whose tongue utters no slander, who does no wrong to a neighbor, and casts no slur on others.

PSALM 15:1–3

Psalm 15 gives a wonderful picture of a place I want to be: a place where people speak truthfully and from their hearts; where there is no lying, where neighbors live in harmony, where people honor and respect each other, where those in power have no time for exploitation or abuse. Sounds great! How do I get in?

God's Holy Hill is that which the human heart most deeply longs for: a place of perfect belonging. Yet, according to this psalm, it is a place that we are distinctly unqualified for. If I were to enter this place, I would ruin it. I hide my true feelings from others; I put on a mask. I know that my thoughts and motives are often selfish, and selfishness destroys belonging.

I can't climb God's Holy Hill myself, but I can acknowledge my inconsistencies. I can be open and vulnerable about my failures and allow God's Spirit to deal with them.

Jesus spent His time on earth forging connections with ordinary people who were vulnerable, hurting, inconsistent, and broken. They didn't have to be perfect to be accepted by Him. They just had to respond to His ministry. And Jesus's acceptance brought them to God's Holy Hill, where they could belong perfectly.

Remember the Samaritan woman at the well? She had been rejected by her community for her poor life choices, but Jesus repaired her relationship with her community and her relationship with God. "Many of the Samaritans from that town believed in him because of the woman's testimony, 'He told me everything I ever did' " (John 4:39). Jesus accomplished the woman's rehabilitation by exposing—and purging—her secrets.

- Pray for God's help in taking a small step toward vulnerability today, dropping the mask that requires such an effort to keep up.
- Show compassion toward someone else whose failure has been exposed. They're no different from you!

Come humbly to God's Holy Hill.

3. Cornish Lighthouse Myths – John 3:1—21

This is the verdict: light has come into the world, but people loved darkness instead of light because their deeds were evil. . . . Whoever lives by the truth comes into the light, so that it may be seen plainly that what they have done has been done in the sight of God.

JOHN 3:19, 21

In the days before radar and satellite navigation, ships counted on lighthouses to show them the way and warn them of dangerous stretches of coastline. There's an intriguing myth that Cornish peasants of previous centuries, steeped in poverty and rural isolation on the southwest coast of England, would sometimes place lanterns on the tops of cliffs over treacherous parts of the sea. According to the legend, they were hoping that passing ships, laden with all kinds of useful cargo, would mistake these lights for nearby lighthouses, lose their bearings, and crash on the rocks. The peasants would be waiting, ready to collect any flotsam and jetsam that washed up on the shore from the wreckage. It would have been a brutal way of making a living, and our modern romantic view of the past revels in such stories of those precarious times.

Current research concludes that the "false lighthouse" stories are mostly just that: false. They make for good novels and TV series, but while locals have always scavenged for goods washed up on the beach near them, there is little evidence that they tried to fool ships with lanterns.

In fact, ships steer away from lights to avoid wrecking. And for a lantern to look like a lighthouse, it would have to have been so big that transporting it would have been extremely difficult. Even if such a light could be maneuvered onto a clifftop, it would have attracted the attention of the authorities. That's the last thing ship wreckers would have wanted! [ii]

We need to follow the light of God and not be waylaid by the false lights that are out there. We need to order our lives as wisely as ship captains—being guided by the true lighthouse and avoiding treacherous rocks. How? False lights tend to be bright flashes that fade quickly. They are the fads of the moment, the fifteen-minute celebrities, or the current crisis. Don't be distracted by these. Keep your hearts fixed on God's steady light.

You may know someone who is stumbling through life right now. They need God's light to find their way. We can be reflectors of God's light, and help others to see their way more clearly. God's Word is light, and His followers live in the light. Let's help others navigate a clear path by reflecting God's steady, strong, penetrating light into the dark places of this world.

- Maybe there's a dark corner of your life. Allow God's light in, and relish the freedom and release it gives.
- Try to reflect God's steady light to those around you and help someone who may be stumbling at this time.

Let God's light be your guiding lighthouse.

4. Remain in the Vine – John 15:1–17

"Remain in me, as I also remain in you. No branch can bear fruit by itself; it must remain in the vine. Neither can you bear fruit unless you remain in me. I am the vine; you are the branches. If you remain in me and I in you, you will bear much fruit; apart from me you can do nothing."

JOHN 15:4–5

The disciples of Jesus, gathered together at the Last Supper, would have grown up around vineyards and would have been able to relate to the picture Jesus was painting.

They would have known that vines are vulnerable to pests and diseases. In order to combat these problems, grape farmers employ several techniques. First, they use grafted vines. Branches grafted to hardier root stock make a greater variety of grapes possible in less-than-ideal climates. Second, they grow vines where the soil can drain properly, often on slopes. Excessive moisture can lead to mildew and rot. Vines, unlike other plants, actually struggle to produce fruit in soils that are too rich in nutrients. Third, they space vine plants apart so the leaves don't shade the neighboring vines and cause fungal growth.

We are often "planted" in less-than-ideal situations—in our careers, our families, or our neighborhoods—where we are weak and vulnerable. We are susceptible to distractions, unfruitful periods, and injury. We may not feel we have what we need to cope. That's why we need to remain in Jesus, to be "grafted" to Him and keep turning to Him as our friend and source of strength.

Our challenging situations may drain us at times. We may give our time by helping others, working for the church, or volunteering for charities, only to find ourselves time-poor and exhausted. But like the vines on the slope, drainage is what helps Christians thrive. We flourish when we give of ourselves, not when we are drowning in selfish accumulation. Jesus provides the ultimate example of draining himself for our sakes: "Greater love has no one than this: to lay down one's life for one's friends" (v. 13).

We may find that we are the only Christian in our community, and this can be a lonely experience. But like the vines, we are better spread out. Of course, there are blessed times when we can come together, fellowship together, and support each other. But our faith is strengthened when we go out into the world and share with others God's invitation to belong.

Whichever difficult situation you find yourself in at the moment, know that you belong to Jesus, that you are grafted into Jesus. As you take advantage of His strength, His energy, and His love in the middle of those troubles, you will thrive and flourish.

- Come away from your problems for a moment and thank Jesus for His strength.
- What have you been accumulating too much of? How can you use that for the benefit of others?

"Keep my commands . . . so that my joy may be in you and your joy may be complete" (John 15:10–11).

5. Set Your Thermostat – Ephesians 4:1–16

That the body of Christ may be built up until we all reach unity in the faith and in the knowledge of the Son of God and become mature, . . . no longer infants, tossed back and forth by the waves, and blown here and there by every wind of teaching.

EPHESIANS 4:12–14

What's your household thermostat set at? Here in Britain, with our cool, damp weather, our house is fitted with radiators in each room that are connected to a central boiler. Water is heated by natural gas and circulated through the pipes to warm the house evenly. Our thermostat is set at 68°F (20°C). It's in a fairly central location (the dining room), but even so, the thermostat is not brilliant at regulating the temperature in the whole house.

The dining room is next to the stairs, so a lot of the heat goes straight up to the bedrooms. If we close the dining room door, that room heats up quickly, causing the thermostat to switch off the boiler, and the rest of the house gets cold. Likewise, if we have the oven on in the kitchen, the heat keeps the dining room next door toasty, so the boiler doesn't switch on at all, and we shiver in the living room.

We're often looking for "thermostats" in life: gauges by which to regulate our behavior and measure our success. Often we resort to comparing ourselves to others. *Am I achieving as much as my colleague, neighbor, sister, or church leader?* Or we strive to adhere to a set of prescribed rules. *Have I managed to stick to the latest fad diet, workout routine, or mindfulness program this week?*

These gauges may be helpful to a point, but we need to recognize their shortcomings. Programs and rules, like my house thermostat, don't take into account changing circumstances. Should you beat yourself up just because you missed your run today on account of your daughter's birthday party? And measuring yourself against others is even dicier. People are fickle and unreliable. Their thermostats are "tossed back and forth by the waves."

When you join a club, you may have a simple set of rules to follow, and that's fine within the context of the club. But when you join the family of God, there's only one unchanging, ever-reliable, steady thermostat by which you should be regulated: God's love.

His love gives us the strength we need to do those tasks He has for us. His love gives us confidence and total security. His love supports us unfailingly when we fall down. And His love, unlike everything else in life, never changes. This is the thermostat to set the course of our lives by.

- What are you feeling insecure about right now? Actively pray that God will help you understand His love in that situation.
- Today, show God's love to someone else whose thermostat is unsteady.

Have a God-centered thermostat.

B: Helping Each Other

6. The Zacchaeus Dilemma – Luke 19:1–10

I attended a conference a few months ago. I didn't know anyone else there, and I found myself in that awkward position at lunch, holding my tray and looking for somewhere to sit. Everyone else seemed to be sitting with friends, laughing, and chatting. I didn't want to impose, but I also didn't want to be a "Billy no mates" sitting by herself.

I was so grateful when someone tapped me on the shoulder, said they recognized me from the morning seminar, and invited me to join them. This socially enlightened person then got everyone at the table to introduce themselves, and soon we were all chatting together, having discovered common interests. I'm still in touch with a couple of them.

This may not sound quite like the story of Zacchaeus, but I wonder if it has more parallels than we were taught in Sunday school. The traditional story goes that Zacchaeus, short in stature, short on morals, and short on friends, was a tax collector in Jericho who was curious to see Jesus. He was shunned by the community because of his dishonesty, but Jesus singled him out and got him to confess his sins and pay back all that he had stolen, plus interest.

Why did Jesus invite himself to Zacchaeus's house? From our modern perspective, this seems strange, even rude. But in the culture of that day, travelers expected to be offered food and lodging when they arrived in a new community. Zacchaeus was "wealthy" (v. 2), so he was an obvious choice to do the hosting.

However, we see that the community in Jericho despised Zacchaeus, and when he "welcomed [Jesus] gladly, all the people saw this and began to mutter" (vv. 6–7). The community had ostracized Zacchaeus and weren't happy for him to play the role of host. He was a pariah. Jesus, by requesting hospitality, gave Zacchaeus the opportunity to be a good citizen, to play his role.

And Zacchaeus was so grateful that he became eager to prove that he could be a positive member of the community. He announced, "I [will] give half of my possessions to the poor, and if I have cheated anybody out of anything, I will pay back four times the amount" (v. 8). Was he repenting of all that he had stolen? Or was he simply saying that he had been honest in his dealings, and he didn't fear being charged four times for any theft that could be proven? Either way, he was making a bid to be accepted again.

Jesus said, "Today salvation has come to this house" (v. 9), restoring Zacchaeus to the community. But notice Jesus's next words: "Because this man, too, is a son of Abraham." Was this a rebuke to the rest of the crowd? Jesus seems to be saying, "He's one of you; welcome him as part of your group." Just like that thoughtful person at the conference.

When you see someone on the outside, the temptation is to think they must be strange or different. But avoid this temptation. Instead, invite them in. Give them the opportunity to play their role in the group. Do your bit to "seek and save the lost" (v. 10).

- The next time you are in a group, look out for the person on the fringe. Invite them to take part.
- If you find yourself on the fringe, remind yourself that you are fully accepted in the worldwide community of believers.

Welcome in the stranger.

7. Extravagant Wisdom – Proverbs 8:12–21

Who is wise and understanding among you? Let them show it by their good life, by deeds done in the humility that comes from wisdom. But if you harbor bitter envy and selfish ambition in your hearts, do not boast about it or deny the truth. Such "wisdom" does not come down from heaven but is earthly, unspiritual, demonic. For where you have envy and selfish ambition, there you find disorder and every evil practice.

But the wisdom that comes from heaven is first of all pure; then peace-loving, considerate, submissive, full of mercy and good fruit, impartial and sincere. Peacemakers who sow in peace reap a harvest of righteousness.

JAMES 3:13–18

Wisdom "that comes from heaven" is what we need to form healthy relationships that are "pure, peace-loving, considerate, submissive, full of mercy and good fruit, impartial and sincere." Isn't this what we all want?

The book of Proverbs talks a lot about God's wisdom and the need to pursue it. "I, wisdom, dwell together with prudence" (PROVERBS 8:12). Prudence, then, is important as we strive to be wise. Prudence is being modest, cautious, and careful in our use of resources.

And yet, as I write this, there is the most glorious sunrise outside my window. Pink, red, orange, and pale blue strokes sweep across the sky in ever-changing arcs. It's anything but prudent. I'd call it *extravagant*! God is lavish in His generosity and creativity. He holds the resources of the universe. In fact, He has the resources to create more universes, and perhaps He already has!

In God, the Omnipotent and Omniscient, wisdom dwells with extravagance. Wisdom, in Proverbs 8:13, goes on to say, "I hate pride and arrogance." Perhaps we, as mortals, need to embrace prudence in a way that God doesn't. Our human efforts to be extravagant often lead to pride and arrogance. James, in his letter, describes this as "envy and selfish ambition."

The writer of Proverbs gives us the results of combining wisdom with prudence: riches, honor, prosperity, righteousness and justice (8:18–21). As we understand what is meant by heavenly wisdom, as opposed to human wisdom, we will be able to exercise righteous extravagance toward each other—the extravagance that is pure, peace-loving, considerate, submissive, full of mercy and good fruit, impartial, and sincere.

- Ask God to show you His wisdom in your upcoming activities.
- Be thankful for God's extravagant creativity and be on the lookout for it today.

Seek the wisdom that comes from heaven.

8. Digging for the Kingdom – Matthew 13

Did you know that elephants dig? Maybe you've seen nature programs with elephants scraping at the ground with their formidable tusks or kicking up clouds of dust with their coffee-table-size feet. But did you know that their digging is hugely beneficial to other animals and plants? When they dig to find water, they create watering holes for other animals in their shared habitat. When they bulldoze a trail through dense forest, they make paths for smaller animals to follow and open up clearings for new plants to grow. In effect, they till the soil.

"Listen then to what the parable of the sower means. . . . The seed falling among the thorns refers to someone who hears the word, but the worries of this life and the deceitfulness of wealth choke the word, making it unfruitful. But the seed falling on good soil refers to someone who hears the word and understands it. This is the one who produces a crop, yielding a hundred, sixty or thirty times what was sown."

MATTHEW 13:18, 22–23

Jesus used tilled soil as an analogy for our relationship with Him. When we communicate with Him regularly, listen to what He has to say to us, and put His words into action, our lives are like plants growing in fertile ground—bountiful and productive.

But when communication between us and Jesus is patchy, or we are distracted by other things in life, or we simply refuse to listen, our lives resemble plants trying to survive on rocky or weed-infested land. We struggle to find a way forward, and every day is a huge, joyless effort.

The lesson is to keep close to Jesus and pay attention to His teachings.

But what about those around us who are struggling? We may be blessed with a strong faith, and we should be thankful if we find ourselves in that good, rich earth. Our gratitude can be expressed by digging. Digging watering holes for others. Digging paths that help them find their way to the good soil.

Let's remember those who find themselves in rocky situations, or those who are so keen to follow Jesus but have trouble keeping focused. Let's show compassion to those who are so burdened by problems that they have lost the joy of living. Let's pray for people who face bullying in the workplace, discrimination, illness, or bereavement. We may not be able to provide neat answers for them, but we can supply friendship, companionship, a listening ear, and a safe place to go. We can till the ground around them, giving them the opportunity to come closer to Jesus themselves.

- Think of someone you can get alongside today.
- Pray for people in your local church or charities who are reaching out to vulnerable people through food banks, homeless shelters, day care centers, and other projects.

Help others find their way to the rich soil of the Kingdom.

9. Who Doesn't Belong? – Romans 12:9–21

Bless those who persecute you; bless and do not curse. Rejoice with those who rejoice; mourn with those who mourn. Live in harmony with one another. Do not be proud, but be willing to associate with people of low position. Do not be conceited.

ROMANS 12:14–16

At the 1988 Olympic Games in Seoul, Canadian sailor Lawrence Lemieux was moving along at a quick clip, even though the seas were exceptionally rough. About halfway through the race, he was in second position and catching up to the leader.

But then, Lemieux heard the cries of two Singaporean sailors nearby. One of them was clinging desperately to his boat, which had capsized under the six-foot waves. The other had drifted fifty feet away, swept off by the currents. Instead of staying in the race, Lemieux set course for the sailors and pulled them out of the water. Lemieux then waited for rescue boats to arrive and finished the race in twenty-third place.

Lemieux missed out on an Olympic medal because he realized that his rivals weren't his enemies. And Lemieux's bravery did not go unrewarded. The Olympic Committee gave him the Pierre de Coubertin medal, a special award for sportsmanship.

It's human nature to define ourselves by who *doesn't* belong to "our team." The problem is that this scrutiny tends to make our group smaller and smaller, as we eliminate more and more people who are different, odd, on the fringes, or just not on our wavelength.

God's group is large—it includes *us*, thankfully! And part of belonging is acknowledging this. As Paul reminds us in the passage from Romans 12, those who belong include those who persecute us, those who triumph over us, those in low positions, and those we would normally think of as enemies.

Actually, realizing that EVERYONE is loved by God and is worthy of our respect is freeing. We don't have to assess people for their worthiness; just show kindness. And caring for someone who treats us badly isn't weakness; it is wielding a weapon that evil does not possess.

- Take a deliberate decision today to offer kindness to someone who doesn't deserve it.
- Thank God that He loves you enough to include you in His group!

No one is unworthy of your kindness.

10. Practice Hospitality – Acts 16:16–40

Xenia is the Greek word for "guest-friendship," and is the root of *xenophobia*, meaning "fear of guests" or "fear of outsiders." *Xenia* is the ancient custom of offering hospitality to strangers. In order to impress on his listeners the importance of providing travelers with a meal and a bed, the Roman poet Ovid (43 BC–17 AD), told the story of Philemon and Baucis. This poor, elderly couple offered a simple meal to two traveling strangers. The travelers were grateful, as they had been refused hospitality at all the other homes in the village. It turned out that the two men were gods in disguise, Zeus and Hermes, who rewarded Philemon and Baucis, but destroyed the rest of the village.

This is the background to Paul and Barnabas's embarrassing encounter with the people of Lystra in Acts 14. The two apostles had entered the city to preach the Good News of Jesus, but after they had healed a man who was lame, the crowd started shouting, " 'The gods have come down to us in human form!' Barnabas they called Zeus, and Paul they called Hermes" (vv. 11, 12). The people were keen to offer them hospitality in hopes of great reward, but Paul said, " 'We too are only human, like you. We are bringing you good news, telling you to turn from these worthless things to the living God' " (v. 15). Even so, Paul and Barnabas had trouble stopping the people from sacrificing to them.

A couple of chapters later, we read an altogether more wholesome story of hospitality. Paul and Silas were thrown into prison for healing a demon-possessed girl. That night, an earthquake destroyed the prison and allowed them to escape. However, instead of escaping, they shared the Good News with the prison warden, who responded joyfully to the message and took them into his house. His motive was not reward from supposed gods but acknowledgement of the one true God, and joyful acceptance of His message.

Giving and accepting hospitality brings rewards and is a response to God's loving acceptance of us. Sharing a meal together is one of the best ways of building community. It doesn't have to be a fancy dinner party, and it doesn't have to be perfect. Paul, in his letter to the Romans, urges us to "*practice* hospitality" (12:13, emphasis added). The more we practice, the better we get at it, and the easier it becomes!

- Who can you invite to share a simple meal with you in your home?
- Think of ways of sharing hospitality: a bring-and-share meal, a boardgames night, a BYOPT (bring-your-own-pizza-toppings) evening, a progressive supper . . . be creative!

Hospitality builds community.

C: Equality in Diversity

11. The Spirit Level – Isaiah 26

You will keep in perfect peace those whose minds are steadfast, because they trust in you. Trust in the LORD forever, for the LORD, the LORD himself, is the Rock eternal.

He humbles those who dwell on high, he lays the lofty city low; he levels it to the ground and casts it down to the dust. Feet trample it down—the feet of the oppressed, the footsteps of the poor.

The path of the righteous is level; you, the Upright One, make the way of the righteous smooth.

ISAIAH 26:3–7

At the beginning of a building project, two surveyors will mark out the area using an optical level. This instrument— a telescope-like device on a tripod—is placed in the center of the area to be surveyed, and posts are placed at strategic points around the edges. One surveyor looks through the eyepiece, which contains a highly accurate bubble level, or spirit level, and guides the other surveyor to mark points on the posts that line up horizontally. To create a level surface for the building, the builders use the markings to dig into terrain that is too high and build up the areas that are too low.

Bible study and prayer can be likened to a surveyor's level. As we read and pray, listening to the Spirit's counsel, we can see where there is unevenness in our lives and in our community. We can take part in God's work of "leveling." He might need to dig into our lives, which can be painful, or He might need to build us up, to boost our confidence.

As you listen carefully and pay attention to God's words, humble yourself to His digging, where necessary. There may be things we need to remove from our lives: unhelpful habits, discouraging thoughts, or unproductive anxieties. At the same time, be prepared for God to encourage you in areas where you are too timid, reluctant, or modest. If someone gives you a compliment, take it as a sign of God's approval and accept it with delight. If you dismiss the compliment, you'll miss out on your blessing, and so will the compliment-giver!

Are there aspects of our community God needs to dig out: fear, inequality, discrimination, or scars from past injuries? We need to acknowledge these, and then work prayerfully with God to remove them. Perhaps there are people or groups in our community who are disadvantaged by life and need building up. Let's be sensitive to God's leading as He directs us to give others a boost.

- Can you pinpoint an anxiety that keeps going around in your head? Ask God to help you dig it out.
- Who can you build up today? Give someone a compliment or a helping hand.

God's work of leveling makes our community smooth.

12. Creative Differences – Philippians 2:1–11

Therefore if you have any encouragement from being united with Christ, if any comfort from his love, if any common sharing in the Spirit, if any tenderness and compassion, then make my joy complete by being like-minded, having the same love, being one in spirit and of one mind.

PHILIPPIANS 2:1–2

I've been working on a charity committee for a while and really appreciate the bonds that have developed as a result. Working together on a project brings people closer together than just meeting up for coffee. (Of course, meeting up for coffee is great for relationships too!) You share struggles and successes. You commiserate and celebrate with each other over your common task.

However, one member of the committee can be a little awkward. He's a nice person in general, hardworking and committed to the project, but has a habit of "sticking a spanner in the works,"—clogging up the system with a problem that wasn't there before. It can be annoying. There we are, making excellent progress, thinking we've covered all our bases and are ready to proceed with action, when he raises an objection, pointing out a potential flaw.

The rest of us don't want to be bothered with this negativity; we want to get on with the project. But over the years, I've learned to value this person's insight. He comes at it from a different perspective. Sometimes it's just a matter of considering his suggestion carefully and dealing with it quickly. Other times, he's saved us from making big mistakes because we'd failed to spot a major omission.

It's good to mix with people who are different from you: people from different backgrounds, age groups, denominations, faiths, cultures, levels of education, job sectors, etc. They can be challenging to get to know and often push us outside our comfort zone. But that is a bonus! They cause us to think in ways we wouldn't if we just stayed in our comfortable clique of like-minded people. They enhance our creativity and may come up with solutions that would never occur to us.

When I'm in a social situation, I try (when I'm feeling brave enough) to seek out someone very different from me. It is sometimes a challenge to make conversation, but I start by simply asking them about themselves: their background, work, family, and experiences. Most people enjoy talking about themselves, and I've learned so much. I've often been humbled by the deep faith of a person I had previously dismissed as shallow or ineffective. And I've sometimes had to reconsider my own long-held prejudices.

- The next time you're at a social gathering, try to seek out the person most different from you and get to know them.
- Thank God for the diversity in your faith community and pray for someone in that group you find difficult to understand.

Differences of opinion can be springboards to creative solutions.

13. The Quilting Challenge – Isaiah 41:11–20

Patchwork quilts have a long tradition in my family. I have a much-loved and much-used quilt that my grandmother made for me many years ago. When she gave it to me, I was surprised to recognize patches from the same material as some of my grandmother's dresses. There were even scraps of material from a dress I'd sewn for myself the previous year. My mother must have given her the leftovers.

These pieces of fabric have different patterns and colors: flowers, stripes, plaid, checks, red, green, brown, yellow, and pink. And yet, my grandmother was clever enough to piece them together in such a way that they make a pleasing whole. The red pieces, with various patterns, make up one big square; the yellow pieces another, and so on. The quilt is framed with light green fabric and backed with a single piece of cotton printed with delicate little flowers. My grandmother was careful to choose a backing piece that complemented the quilt, even though we don't see it most of the time.

How does God piece us together in community to make a pleasing whole? We are all so different. We jostle against each other with our opinions, attitudes, and habits clashing more than a badly chosen outfit.

God the Father lovingly accepts each one of us, even those whom society has discarded as left over or useless. He places us together where He knows we will benefit each other and the whole community.

Most of us choose a group of believers to worship with that we feel comfortable among. They are like the big squares on my quilt: complementary and cohesive. And yet, the scraps that make up those squares are different in pattern

42

and texture. They work together as they become part of the whole quilt.

The quilt is unified by the frame, a solid piece of light green. Jesus is our frame. His uniting work on the cross dissolves all animosities. He doesn't take away the differences, but His love holds us all together. He gives each of us a place, meaning, and purpose.

The single piece of fabric backing the quilt is like the Holy Spirit. He is in every believer and encourages each of us. He backs us up and is the same Holy Spirit throughout the world. He is always there, even though we can't see Him in a physical sense—just as we don't see the back of the quilt as it lies on the bed.

I will put in the desert the cedar and the acacia, the myrtle and the olive. I will set junipers in the wasteland, the fir and the cypress together, so that people may see and know, may consider and understand, that the hand of the LORD has done this, that the Holy One of Israel has created it.

ISAIAH 41:19–20

- Thank the Lord for those you've been "arbitrarily" put next to: your neighbors, colleagues, fellow church workers, and family.
- Thank the Lord that He considers you useful; the "quilt" wouldn't be complete without you!

Jesus brings diversity together in a united whole.

14. Doodling or Scribbling? – Colossians 2:6–19

See to it that no one takes you captive through hollow and deceptive philosophy, which depends on human tradition and the elemental spiritual forces of this world rather than on Christ. For in Christ all the fullness of the Deity lives in bodily form, and in Christ you have been brought to fullness.

COLOSSIANS 2:8–10

Sometimes it feels like we're living dual lives: living by the world's standards in our day-to-day activities and then rejoicing in the freedom we have in Christ when we worship together with fellow believers. The switch can be exhausting!

Freedom, as expressed in Paul's letter to the Colossians, includes freedom from each other's expectations—whether those expectations come from believers or non-believers.

Even in our Christian family, we will find different answers to the big questions. We will worship in different ways; respond to society's challenges in different ways; view marriage, politics, human sexuality, environmental concerns, consumerism, and even militarism differently.

We need to allow each other to find different answers, and not judge. We are all on the journey, and we are all at different places on the journey. Some of us have followed Jesus for years; some for just a short time. The only essential thing is that we are all pursuing a closer relationship with Jesus Christ.

My friend showed me her Bible notes recently. They were doodles and drawings and rainbows and hearts! When I make notes in my Bible or study book, it's all underlines, questions, and bulleted points. Are my Bible studies more worthwhile? Absolutely not! It's just that my mind organizes information differently than hers. Actually, I admired how colorful she had made her Bible. (It was a special "doodlers" Bible, with extra-wide margins—what a fantastic idea!) It was inspiring to look at. My scribblings are more orderly, but boring.

Our belonging is not dependent on falling in line with others, no matter how "holy" or "spiritual" they may be. Our belonging is solely dependent on our relationship with Christ. "In Christ you have been brought to fullness" (v. 10). If Christ accepts us—and He DOES if we just ask—then there is no way we can be more fully accepted into His family. He is the head "from whom the whole body, supported and held together by its ligaments and sinews, grows as God causes it to grow" (v. 19).

So continue to grow into who God made you to be, not depending on anyone else's assessment, and not needing to assess anyone else's worth. Recognize that some of us doodle, and some of us scribble.

- Thank Jesus that He made you and accepts you just as you are.
- Is there a fellow believer whose actions or opinions you disagree with? Let go of judgment, and purpose to engage with them as beloved children of God.

Be freed from judgment and from judging others.

15. The Tango We Dance – Exodus 4:1–17

Moses said to the LORD, "Pardon your servant, Lord. I have never been eloquent, neither in the past nor since you have spoken to your servant. I am slow of speech and tongue." The LORD said to him, "Who gave human beings their mouths? Who makes them deaf or mute? Who gives them sight or makes them blind? Is it not I, the LORD? Now go; I will help you speak and will teach you what to say."

EXODUS 4:10–12

Like Moses, I'm a wallflower-type: happier not to stand out in a group, yet anxious to be acknowledged and affirmed. It's a difficult position to maintain! I'd rather observe than be observed, and in my observations, I draw conclusions about others. I imagine that my observations allow me to understand what they're thinking and feeling. Of course, most of my conclusions have to do with what others are thinking about *me*. Or what I guess they're thinking about me. Quite a self-centered approach.

So, imagine my surprise when, the other day, I was told that someone else felt insecure around me. Someone whose opinion *I* was insecure about. It blew my selfish mind. I was so busy worrying about their opinion of me, I didn't stop to think that they might be anxious about my opinion of *them*.

My desire to fade into the background in groups is not so much Christ-centered humility as self-centered anxiety. If I can observe others from behind a two-way mirror, I can evaluate their behavior and reactions without having to acknowledge my part. I don't have to take responsibility for my effect on them. It's like watching a soap opera and judging the characters' actions. It's fun, entertaining, and divorced from reality.

When sociologists study the behavior of people in groups, they first acknowledge their own influence on the actions of the group. Just by being present, or by setting up a group situation, they realize that they affect how people act.

And this is so true in everyday life. I need to take responsibility for the effect I have on others, even if that effect is unintentional. I need to become more comfortable with the give-and-take of interactions, and with changing perceptions. I know that initial impressions are often wrong and that strong relationships develop over a long period of time. So I shouldn't be unduly upset if the first impression I make is less than perfect. Likewise, I shouldn't take my first impressions of others too seriously, trusting instead that I will get to know individuals better over time.

We all need to be more at ease with the tango we dance around each other as our relationships develop, change, morph, and progress. Giving myself—and others—the benefit of the doubt allows for growth and a more positive approach to belonging.

- Be ready to laugh at yourself when you make a mistake or a mis-judgment today.
- Be more gracious in your evaluation of others and try to give encouragement to someone today.

Leave judgment of others, and of yourself, to God.

D: Resolving Community Problems

16. When Should We Give up? – Gal. 6:1–10

Brothers and sisters, if someone is caught in a sin, you who live by the Spirit should restore that person gently. But watch yourselves, or you also may be tempted. Carry each other's burdens, and in this way you will fulfil the law of Christ. If anyone thinks they are something when they are not, they deceive themselves. Each one should test their own actions. Then they can take pride in themselves alone, without comparing themselves to someone else, for each one should carry their own load. Nevertheless, the one who receives instruction in the word should share all good things with their instructor.

Do not be deceived: God cannot be mocked. A man reaps what he sows. Whoever sows to please their flesh, from the flesh will reap destruction; whoever sows to please the Spirit, from the Spirit will reap eternal life. Let us not become weary in doing good, for at the proper time we will reap a harvest if we do not give up. Therefore, as we have opportunity, let us do good to all people, especially to those who belong to the family of believers.

GALATIANS 6:1–10

For years I struggled to get along with my line manager at work. She was overbearing, insensitive, obnoxious, and even used bad language in the office. It wasn't just me who couldn't stand her; my coworkers complained about her behavior too. Several employees left the firm because they couldn't work with her. I finally resigned and thought my troubles were over.

But God's ways are not my ways. I found myself working for the same company again (through circumstances I won't bore you with here). And I found myself with the same line manager. But somehow, over the course of several months, I started to get to know her as a person rather than just my boss. She actually did have a human side, and we started having little chats together at the end of the day. I found out about her background and some of the burdens she was carrying. That helped me to understand her. I realized that she wasn't insensitive; she just had a different way of expressing her concern for others.

Now, I don't put myself forward as a super spiritual person who never gives up. I did give up. But God didn't. He taught me that everyone, even those we meet in professional or casual circumstances, are of infinite value. No one should be dismissed.

It takes a lot of perseverance to get alongside someone who seems to keep pushing you away. But we have resources that are far beyond our own. And we have a motive that is far beyond anything this world can offer. We have the certain hope of eternal life in God's kingdom. And we know that our efforts to build relationships will have eternal consequences. Surely this is incentive enough to stick with it.

- Is there someone you've given up on, or would like to give up on? Acknowledge their value in God's eyes and look for little ways to value them.
- Thank God for how much He values you, insignificant though you might feel at times.

God will never give up on anyone; nor should we.

17. Build a Strong Dam – Proverbs 17:14–28

Starting a quarrel is like breaching a dam; so drop the matter before a dispute breaks out. . . . The one who has knowledge uses words with restraint, and whoever has understanding is even-tempered.

PROVERBS 17:14, 27

Have you ever had a relationship disintegrate because of a small quarrel? How does that happen? It may not even have been a matter of importance. But somehow it got out of control, and the result was a friendship in tatters or a marriage split.

Life brings disagreements; that is inevitable. We can't avoid having differences of opinion with others. And we will have the most disagreements with those closest to us because we engage with them most frequently. The threat to relationships isn't from disagreements; the threat comes from dealing with them in the wrong way.

In May 2018, Kenya suffered a major tragedy when the Patel Dam collapsed and forty-eight people lost their lives. Engineers rushed to the scene to work out what had gone wrong. The conclusion of Felix Gatumba, a structural engineer working in Kitui, Kenya, was that, during a heavy rainfall, "the strength of the dam might have been compromised after the water levels rose to the brim where the walls are thinnest." He went on to say, "A properly built dam should have a spillway that is below the highest point of the wall, to evacuate excess water during flooding." [iii]

Our interactions in relationships cause the streams that run between us to flow together. Sometimes the waters flow more than we can cope with, and we hold back. We build dams. These relationship dams are actually quite sensible. They stop us from oversharing or being overly dependent. They allow breathing space. But at times, the waters behind the dam surge due to a disagreement that escalates into an argument.

If we haven't allowed for a "spillway"—a structured outlet for our feelings—then the rising waters of our irritation will reach the thin top of our dam, where we are most sensitive, and the dam will be breached. Once that happens, it's hard to stop the flow of anger. We've all experienced it. And it can cause a permanent rift in a relationship.

What does a spillway look like in a relationship? It might be a regular date night, where issues can be talked through in a neutral, distraction-free environment. Or an activity undertaken together, where the focus is not on the dispute, but on achieving a mutual aim. Exercise and fresh air are always useful for letting off steam. For followers of Jesus, worshipping together helps us lift our eyes away from ourselves and onto Him. Make sure you plan some form of re-creation into your life and your relationships.

- Is a relationship in your life going through a rocky patch? Plan an activity to do together.
- Does your daily routine include fresh air and exercise? Reserve time for some outdoor activities!

Don't let a disagreement turn into a dispute.

18. The Tea Strainer – Colossians 3:1–17

Therefore, as God's chosen people, holy and dearly loved, clothe yourselves with compassion, kindness, humility, gentleness and patience. Bear with each other and forgive one another if any of you has a grievance against someone. Forgive as the Lord forgave you. And over all these virtues put on love, which binds them all together in perfect unity.

COLOSSIANS 3:12–14

I have a spoon-shaped tea strainer that I use every day. I fill it with loose-leaf tea—Earl Grey is my favorite—put it in my cup, fill the cup with boiling water and let it steep for several minutes. Then, I empty the tea strainer and leave it on my draining board to dry, ready for the next use. I love it!

After a while, I noticed that the strainer was getting stained. The tannin from the tea was leaving a brown residue, coating the spoon. It wasn't dirty, I told myself; it was the natural effect of the tea leaves, and it didn't really matter that the spoon was becoming dark brown. But finally it was too much, and I decided to give the spoon a good clean. I thought it was permanently stained, but, after some diligent scrubbing, the tannin came off. It is now almost back to its original shine. Why didn't I do that earlier? I've now purposed to give the spoon a light scrub after each use, so that the tannin doesn't build up so much.

Our relationships with others can be like the tea strainer. We bump along together, and little irritations develop and linger like small stains. If we don't deal with them immediately, they can build up and get darker. After a while, they seem to be permanent. *Wasn't that person always difficult? I can never speak openly with him; he*

54

always rebuffs me. I can't trust her with a confidence; she'll just blab it around. And they'll never change. I will just avoid them and keep our interactions superficial.

But is that the best response? Paul urges us, in his letter to the Colossians, not just to tolerate each other but to actively love each other, showing compassion and forgiveness.

In my experience (born out of a host of mistakes!), many irritations, and even long-standing animosities, can be resolved if we approach one another with the right attitude. First, pray for a compassionate heart. Second, listen carefully to the other person, without judging. Then, explain your point of view without blaming the other person. Finally, express your appreciation of the other as a dearly loved brother or sister in Christ.

Once you've scrubbed the relationship and dealt with the big stains, don't let them build up again. Make a habit of letting the person know you appreciate them and care about them. And if there is a minor irritation—which is only natural—deal with it quickly.

- Is there a serious "stain" in your relationship with someone else? Ask God to help you deal with it, using the four steps above.
- Show appreciation toward someone today.

Indifference stains; love remains.

19. Striving to Belong – Proverbs 14:32

Ian Gillan, lead singer for the rock band Deep Purple, said, "A sense of belonging is more important than money." [iv] James Michener, the famous author, said, "The sense of belonging is one of the great gifts men get in battle." [v]

The deep need to belong leads people to join . . . anything. They may try sports clubs, choral societies, charity shops, political parties, or joining up when "their country needs them." Some people try gangs, taking drugs, shoplifting, drinking to excess, destructive workaholic behavior, dieting to the point of anorexia, attempting daredevil stunts, exhaustive volunteering, or even betraying a family member in order to get in with the "right crowd." Often, people do these things not because they are bent on hurting themselves or others, but rather, because they are in pursuit of a sense of belonging. So how can you tell the difference between "destructive" belonging and "constructive" belonging?

When calamity comes, the wicked are brought down, but even in death the righteous seek refuge in God.

PROVERBS 14:32

The writer of this proverb gives us a clue about the difference between a negative and positive effort to belong. Those who have made bad decisions about which group to belong to will be found out when trouble comes. Think about candidates in a political party. The party that seemed so united and strong suddenly comes apart with infighting the day after their election defeat. Or what about an army? Those who are "brothers in arms" will sometimes turn on each other if the battle isn't going in their favor, or if leadership fails. That band that achieved fame and fortune with a number one hit are at each other's throats when money problems arise and personalities clash.

By contrast, those who build their sense of belonging on compassion and care for one another are often brought closer together in moments of crisis. For example, a bereavement may bring about reconciliation and a strengthening of bonds within a family or neighborhood.

Now, joining a political party or music band is not inherently bad; the way relationships are built within the group determines if it is destructive or constructive. Choosing to belong out of selfish ambition is a bad decision, even if it is to a church group or volunteer organization. It will reap heartache.

The MESSAGE paraphrases Proverb 14:32 like this: "The evil of bad people leaves them out in the cold; the integrity of good people creates a safe place for living." Good relationships are built on honesty and vulnerability. We can nurture good relationships by practicing open communication. This is the way to achieve a sense of belonging that will withstand the worst calamities.

- Think of a group you are part of that gives you a sense of belonging. Tell someone in the group how much you value their integrity.
- Think of a group you are part of that struggles to keep it together. How can you start to encourage open communication in this group?

Belonging is more than just group membership.

20. Dealing with Conflict – 1 Timothy 2:1–8

I urge, then, first of all, that petitions, prayers, intercession and thanksgiving be made for all people—for kings and all those in authority, that we may live peaceful and quiet lives in all godliness and holiness.

1 TIMOTHY 2:1–2

Don't take sides.

"There are always two sides," we hear, and it is true. In fact, in any dispute, there are probably more than two sides. And as human beings, we are not likely to be able to see the issue from all sides. We have limited capacities, biases, and prejudices simply because of where we came from and how we were brought up. This is true for disputes between individuals, community-wide problems, and national/international conflicts.

The United Kingdom, where I currently live, has been torn apart by the Brexit issue: whether to remain part of the European Union or not. There are Christians on both sides of the issue—Christians with very strong arguments on both sides; Christians I respect on both sides; Christians at each other's throats over this issue. In many circles, it has become a taboo topic due to the strong feelings it evokes. And many of us wonder, "Which side is God on?"

This is the wrong question. God is always on the side of peace and reconciliation. We see Him at work throughout history in many different political contexts. He was at work within the court of Pharaoh. He worked with the judges of the Old Testament, and He showered His blessings on Israel during the reign of the kings. He brought salvation to the world under the empire of the Romans. He continues

58

to work within democracies, autocracies, theocracies, and dictatorships around the world. His blessings cannot be said to prefer any form of government.

I believe the same is true in personal disputes, as well as moral and theological debates. God loves every one of His children equally. He cares for us all. He sees the bigger picture that we cannot. What is the correct view on homosexuality, abortion, warfare, or capital punishment? We may never agree, but we don't have to. We can leave it to God, who judges perfectly. Isn't that freeing?

Instead of standing up for "our side" or "our rights," our best response in disputes is to listen and try to understand.

- The next time you're asked to choose a side, don't. Work at building relationships with people from both sides.
- When there's a dispute raging around you—in your family, community, or nation—pray about it, but don't judge. Leave that to God.

Let's pray together rather than pull apart.

E: The Community Already Around You

21. Building Together – Nehemiah 12:27–47

At the dedication of the wall of Jerusalem, the Levites were sought out from where they lived and were brought to Jerusalem to celebrate joyfully the dedication with songs of thanksgiving and with the music of cymbals, harps and lyres. . . . So in the days of Zerubbabel and of Nehemiah, all Israel contributed the daily portions for the musicians and the gatekeepers. They also set aside the portion for the other Levites, and the Levites set aside the portion for the descendants of Aaron.

NEHEMIAH 12:27, 47

The Book of Nehemiah describes how a small group of refugees returned to their country after decades of exile and rebuilt their lives. It pays to read the whole book in one sitting (skipping over the lists of names) to see how these haggard, desultory stragglers were transformed into a tight-knit, hardworking team. Nehemiah must have had good leadership skills, but he gives the glory to God: "So the wall [of Jerusalem] was completed on the twenty-fifth of Elul, in fifty-two days. When all our enemies heard about this, all the surrounding nations were afraid and lost their self-confidence, because they realized that this work had been done with the help of our God" (6:15–16).

Throughout the story, Nehemiah describes how each family, or clan, was given a different section of Jerusalem's wall to repair. And a variety of skills were needed to support the rebuilding. There were stonemasons, metal workers, carpenters, roofers, watchmen, gatekeepers, farmers, and vintners.   Those who had plenty shared with those who had little. Each gave what they could of their time, energy, money, and provisions. As the wall went up, the people's confidence increased.

Nehemiah also describes the problems the refugees encountered. Sometimes those problems came from outside, but sometimes they were caused by disagreements or greed within the group. Nehemiah repeatedly reminded them why they were rebuilding, that they needed each other, and that they needed to be mindful of God's laws— the laws that make community. When the people acknowledged their mistakes, they were able to come together again and be healed. When they finished rebuilding, they thanked God, reminded themselves of His laws, and sang joyously together.

What a wonderful picture of belonging! Each doing what they could and giving what they had for the greater good. God's kingdom is built like this. God entrusts each of us with something—whether a little or a lot doesn't matter. When we use what He gives us to build up the community, it becomes something more. Our confidence in Him grows, and our sense of belonging is strengthened.

- What do you have to contribute to your community? Thank God for how you are able to help, even in a small way, in building His kingdom.
- Acknowledge that you cannot build your life by yourself, and give thanks for the community that God has placed you in at this time.

Use what you have where you have been placed.

22. Communal Responsibility – Luke 10:25–37

"Love the Lord your God with all your heart and with all your soul and with all your strength and with all your mind; and love your neighbor as yourself."

LUKE 10:27

In our individualistic society, we grow up learning to take responsibility for ourselves. *I need to study hard so that I can get a good job in order to support myself and not be a burden on society. I need to make decisions for myself, not wait for others to make them for me. I need to take care of my own health so that others don't have to take care of me.*

This is useful to a certain extent, but we often go too far and forget our communal responsibility. The great religions and philosophies of the world agree that we are responsible not just for our own well-being but also for the well-being of our whole community.

Confucius taught about the five key relationships and the principle of "Li": there should be love and respect between ruler and subject, father and son, husband and wife, elder and younger, and friend and friend.

Judaism teaches that we should constantly improve our efforts to alleviate the crises that affect others. They refer to the allegorical practice of *eglah arufah*, or "broken-necked heifer." When a person is found dead in the wilderness and the killer is not known, the elders of the closest city take a heifer and break its neck as an offering for their forgiveness and to establish their innocence. They take responsibility for the death because it is believed that their community had not provided sufficient care and concern for the individual who perished so tragically. Had they embraced this person with food, shelter, and support, an undignified death could have been avoided. [vi]

Islam emphasizes the individual's responsibility to the community, and the community's responsibility to the individual. The prophet Mohammed told a parable about people who drew lots for their seats in a boat. Some of them got seats in the front part and the others in the back. When the latter needed water, they had to go up to the front to fetch it, so they said, "Let us make a hole in our share of the ship to get water, saving us from troubling those at the front." If the people in the front left the others to do what they had suggested, all the people of the ship would be destroyed. But if those at the front helped those at the back, both parties would be safe. [vii]

There can be no greater example to us of communal responsibility than Jesus's parable of the Good Samaritan. The Samaritan man recognized his responsibility toward the injured victim on the road, even though he was from a different religious group. Read this well-known story again, from the Gospel of Luke, and ask yourself the same question as that expert in Jewish law: "Who is my neighbor?"

- Who is your neighbor? Write a list as God prompts you.
- Make an effort to make contact with your "neighbors," one by one.

Take responsibility for the community where God has placed you.

23. Triangulation – 1 Corinthians 3:1–15

You are still worldly. For since there is jealousy and quarreling among you, are you not worldly? Are you not acting like mere humans? For when one says, "I follow Paul," and another, "I follow Apollos," are you not mere human beings? What, after all, is Apollos? And what is Paul? Only servants, through whom you came to believe—as the Lord has assigned to each his task. I planted the seed, Apollos watered it, but God has been making it grow.

1 CORINTHIANS 3:3–6

If you want to pinpoint your location accurately, you can use a method known as triangulation. You make a triangle between yourself, another known point, and a celestial body. Then, through a series of complicated calculations, you can measure the angles between these three points and determine your exact position.

We are often amused by ancient maps, which portray countries and continents in comical proportions, but triangulation techniques weren't standardized until the eighteenth century. Using the sun and the stars to measure distances was already common in ancient times. The astrolabe was brought to Europe by Arab scientists in the eleventh century, and the sextant came into use around the seventeenth century. But it was monumentally difficult to get consistently accurate calculations. Different countries and regions used different techniques and got interestingly different results. Nowadays, we use GPS. This highly sophisticated technology is still based on the premise of using three points to determine position, but the celestial bodies used these days are man-made satellites.

In his letter to the Corinthian church, Paul expresses dismay at their relationships with each other: "There is jealousy and quarreling among you" (v. 3). He diagnoses their problem: they are looking to other people—Paul or Apollos—to determine their relationships instead of looking to God.

Healthy relationships are built when we take time to get to know each other, and as we learn to know God together. If we leave God out of our relationships, if we don't "triangulate with a celestial body," our measurements of each other will be inaccurate. That's how jealousy and quarreling seep in.

Paul goes on to talk about Jesus Christ being the foundation of the building. That building is the kingdom of God, and we are part of it as we grow together in the knowledge of God and His love for us. Jesus Christ laid the firm base for our relationships when He made the way to God.

As we build our relationships with each other, let's look up to the heavens, to God, to determine our positions within the Kingdom. Don't rely on others to give you an accurate evaluation of your standing. Rely on God's viewpoint.

- God gives each of us a firm base in His kingdom through Jesus Christ. Rejoice in that certainty.
- View the next person you meet from God's perspective.

Measure your relationships by looking to God.

24. The Closest Place to God – Acts 17:16–31

Where is the closest place to God? This is an important question, given the focus on triangulation in study 23. If developing closer relationships with others depends on being close to God, where is He? And how can I get there? Especially when I feel far away from Him?

From one man he made all the nations, that they should inhabit the whole earth; and he marked out their appointed times in history and the boundaries of their lands. God did this so that they would seek him and perhaps reach out for him and find him, though he is not far from any one of us. "For in him we live and move and have our being." As some of your own poets have said, "We are his offspring."

ACTS 17:26–31

Take String Theory. This is a very advanced and complicated set of hypotheses that physicists are working on at the moment. Albert Einstein and his colleagues started thinking along these lines, and Stephen Hawking took it up with gusto, hoping to find a "Theory of Everything." I don't understand the complexities of it in the least, but the basics of string theory may help us understand God's presence.

One hypothesis of string theory is that there are more dimensions in the universe than the three we can measure. In order to understand this concept, imagine an MRI scan of someone's brain. We "see" the whole of someone's brain as individual "slices." We know that the brain is not any one of those slices, or even all the slices put together, but a unified whole that the slices represent. Our three-dimensional minds can make sense of the two-dimensional pictures. But our minds are simply not able to take in the universe with its ten dimensions (in addition to time) that physicists are now postulating. [viii]

This is all very interesting, but what does it have to do with God?

Einstein, working on this theory of multiple dimensions, suggested that all forces are different manifestations of a single grand unified force, and that there is one Large Dimension that encompasses all the other sets of dimensions. They all work together and interact. [ix]   In spiritual terms, God is the Large Dimension within which all the other dimensions were created. We live in the physical universe with its multiple dimensions, but we can only measure, and science can only tell us about, those dimensions that we can perceive.

So God is everywhere. God creates everything that exists and is the source of all things. And all of creation and God interact, but some parts are hidden from us, or partly hidden from us. We can't relate to God as a separate being, as if God were standing in front of us. We can love the presence of God that is all around us. And as an aid to those of us who only work in three dimensions, God sent Jesus, who was—and is—God Himself, and allowed us to observe His life.

- Close your eyes for five minutes and enjoy the parts of creation that science can't describe.
- Thank God for His constant presence in you, around you, in everything, and around everything.

God is everywhere; outside of God there is nothing.

25. The Thin, Slippery Rope – 1 Cor. 1:18–25

For the message of the cross is foolishness to those who are perishing.

1 CORINTHIANS 1:18

Well, of course, it is! The message of the cross is about letting go, surrendering our self-assurance, and putting our assurance in something that seems to lead to death.

Bill Nighy, a well-known British actor, was recently interviewed in *The Observer* newspaper. He is generally regarded as a suave, laconic, self-assured man with a snappy dress-sense. In fact, he admits he is nothing of the sort. In real life he describes himself as fretful, under-confident and deeply self-critical. He hates watching himself in films and won't even read his own interviews. If he does catch a glimpse of himself on screen, it takes him a long time to recover. He explains, "It's because all my fears about my inadequacies are confirmed when I watch myself." [x]

Bill Nighy is desperate to hide from his fears, and many of us feel the same way. Unfortunately, this desperation pulls us away from others and isolates us.

It's as though you're dangling on a rope, clinging to it for dear life. Anyone who suggests that you let go is crazy! You're struggling with all your might just to hold on to what little confidence you have. You grasp at other ropes that might be nearby—friends, money, job status, therapy, self-help gurus—and even clamber over others in your panic to save yourself.

But where are you climbing *to*? The top of the rope does not represent the firm ground you hope for; Bill Nighy has made it to the top of his profession, yet he feels insecure. At the top of your rope is just thinner rope. And if you do make it to the top, you'll have an even longer way to fall.

If only you could see that under you, at the bottom, are the vast, safe, strong arms of Jesus, who Himself "let go" and surrendered to the cross. In doing this, He conquered the depths.

Jews demand signs and Greeks look for wisdom, but we preach Christ crucified: a stumbling-block to Jews and foolishness to Gentiles, but to those whom God has called, both Jews and Greeks, Christ the power of God and the wisdom of God. For the foolishness of God is wiser than human wisdom, and the weakness of God is stronger than human strength.

1 CORINTHIANS 1:22–25

Letting go of the precarious ropes we cling to doesn't lead to our destruction. It enables us to connect with others instead of competing with them for rope space. We are secure when we are on the firm ground at the bottom, safe in God's love. Our hands are free, and we can reach out to each other.

- Who are you in competition with? Make a gesture of camaraderie with that person today.
- Have you set a target or goal for yourself that feeds your insecurity? Let go and focus on the people around you instead.

Letting go of the things to which we cling is the way to safety.

F: Rejoicing Together

26. Being on the Winning Team – Psalm 126

I'm not a great sports fan, but even I was caught up in the national excitement here in the UK when the women's football (soccer!) team won a surprise victory over the favorites, Japan, in the SheBelieves Cup final of 2019.

England was considered the underdog going into the tournament, having been knocked out the previous year by the USA. To everyone's surprise, they progressed to the final. But then they faced Japan, a team they'd last played, and lost to, in 2015. Two of their players were out due to injury, and another had just come back from rehab. It was a David and Goliath match.

The celebration when they defeated Japan 3–0 was spectacular, made all the more so by their obvious disbelief and wonderment. There were scenes of teammates hugging, crying, jumping in the air, and then fans joining in to congratulate the team.

Team manager Phil Neville was asked about his recipe for success, and the togetherness of the group was one of his answers. Another was giving every player the chance to play in the final. Steph Houghton, one of those called to play toward the end, said, "We call ourselves The Finishers. We're not The Bench; we're there to back up anything that's going on and have a positive impact." [xi]

Goalscorer Lucy Staniforth, who started for the first time, agreed that being made to feel valued was a big part of the squad's success. Leah Williamson added, "This is the toughest game I've played in an England shirt. I'm just really happy today to have survived and win a trophy." [xii] The triumph continued as the squad arrived back in the UK to jubilant crowds, parades, and TV interviews.

When the LORD restored the fortunes of Zion, we were like those who dreamed. Our mouths were filled with laughter, our tongues with songs of joy.... Those who go out weeping, carrying seed to sow, will return with songs of joy, carrying sheaves with them.

PSALM 126:1–2, 6

Christians are part of the winningest team in history, although we're often considered the underdogs. Jesus has already won the greatest match for us when He defeated death. The triumph and joy when we finally ascend the Lord's Hill and come into His kingdom will be unsurpassed. All our trials, failures, sorrows, and defeats will be nothing compared to the jubilation that will carry on forever.

And we will share this joy together, as each member of the team is just as valuable as the other. We will ascend the Lord's Hill, hand in hand, with laughter and songs. What a picture! Let's rejoice!

- What personal defeat is getting you down at the moment? View it from the context of the ultimate win.
- Look around at your fellow teammates. Each one of them will share with you in the final victory, and you will share with them.

God's kingdom is a sure victory.

27. Dry Stone Walls – Ephesians 2:14–22

You are no longer foreigners and strangers, but fellow citizens with God's people and also members of his household, built on the foundation of the apostles and prophets, with Christ Jesus himself as the chief cornerstone. In him the whole building is joined together and rises to become a holy temple in the Lord. And in him you too are being built together to become a dwelling in which God lives by his Spirit.

EPHESIANS 2:19–22

Dry stone walls are a common feature in the countryside near where I live. They are a traditional method of constructing a barrier, usually to keep livestock in and predators out. On the hills of Dartmoor, where trees are scarce, they are a clever way of using what nature provides. Land users would dig stones out of the fields they wanted to cultivate and pile them up on the side. They would then fit the stones carefully together to construct a wall, using no mortar or other binding substance. Some dry walls have survived for hundreds of years.

When we go hiking, we often come across walls that are crumbling, mossy, covered in brambles, and pierced with trees that have made them their foundation. They are beautiful. But why do we find these old, dilapidated structures appealing?

They are a testament to strenuous work and the dedication of past generations of land users. They have stood the test of time. Their strength lies in the skill of the builder slotting each stone into place with the next. The creepers and climbers that have made their homes in the wall soften it, settling it into the countryside, absorbing the wall as part of the earth. The trees that spring out of the wall are supported by it, and they in turn hold the stones together with their roots, forming an organic, symbiotic relationship.

Likewise, we have been slotted into families, churches, communities, workplaces, and organizations. We often rub uncomfortably against each other. Challenges spring up between us and threaten to push us apart. But those same challenges can strengthen us as we work through our differences and come up with new ways of being together. This process takes time and determination. If we commit our efforts to the Lord, it will result in a beautiful structure—organic with its lumps and bumps, elegant with its warts and scars.

Make the effort to pray together with those in your family, church or community group. Commit yourselves to each other with God's help.

- Note the variety of people that make up your church or faith community. List the range of ages, family groupings, ethnic backgrounds, professions, political leanings, and worship preferences.
- Embrace the irritations that come with being part of a community. If handled well, they can become seeds of beauty.

There is such beauty in God's communities.

28. Praying Together – Acts 4:1–36

"Now, Lord, consider their threats and enable your servants to speak your word with great boldness. Stretch out your hand to heal and perform signs and wonders through the name of your holy servant Jesus." After they prayed, the place where they were meeting was shaken. And they were all filled with the Holy Spirit and spoke the word of God boldly.

ACTS 4:29–31

Reading how the early Christians prayed together makes me feel very inadequate! Somehow, they caught a vision of the Kingdom that enabled them to pray it into happening. And consider the context of their prayers.

Peter and John had just been arrested and thrown into prison. They'd upset the Jewish authorities in Jerusalem by proclaiming some new religion, based on a charismatic leader who'd been put to death by the Romans only months earlier. These troublemakers were saying that their religious guru, a man called Jesus of Nazareth, had come back to life. And they'd just backed up their claims by healing a man who'd been lame. The healing was undisputed; everyone in Jerusalem knew about the annoying beggar with shriveled legs who'd sat in front of the temple every day. Now the crowds were starting to drift over to this new religion, and the Jewish leaders saw their power waning.

To add insult to injury, these uneducated country hicks were saying that the Jewish authorities themselves were to blame for Jesus's death. The people were turning against them. To salvage the situation, the authorities decided to release Peter and John, but only after warning them not to speak of this Jesus, or their new religion, again.

Peter and John were restored to the growing Christian community, whose response was to pray together. And did they pray that God would protect them from the authorities? That God would remove the power of those leaders? That God would give the Christians an escape route?

No, they prayed for *boldness*. They prayed that they would be able to proclaim the Good News of Jesus and His kingdom more and more. And they prayed for more healings and miracles—the very things that had gotten them into trouble in the first place!

God answered their prayers in astonishing ways. He didn't take away all trouble; the story of Acts is filled with persecution of the early church. But the end of chapter 4 describes the community of God at its best: they shared what they had, they cared for each other, they were united in heart and mind, and they became a powerful witness to the world.

May our prayers together be so bold!

- The next time you pray together with fellow believers, consider what you are praying for. Are you asking to be taken out of a difficult situation? Or are you asking to be given the resources you need to deal with the difficult situation in a Christlike way?
- Give thanks for the encouragement of praying together.

Pray for resources, not escape.

29. Acrostic – Psalm 34

Psalm 34 is written as an "acrostic"—a poem in which the first word of each line starts with the next letter of the alphabet. The original was written using the letters of the Hebrew alphabet. The psalm is so comforting, I've written a paraphrase using the English alphabet.

A lleluia! Glorify the Lord with words and singing!

B oast of the Lord's goodness to those in trouble.

C ome together to praise the Lord!

D rawing near to God helped me hear His voice;

E ven my fears receded when I listened to Him.

F aces shine when we raise our eyes to Him.

G round down by worries, I cried out to the Lord;

H e heard, and saved me from all my troubles!

I am comforted by His angel encamped around me;

J ust when I need Him, He delivers me.

K issed by the Lord, I taste His goodness;

L et those who fear Him take refuge in Him.

M ay you seek the Lord and know His provision;

N o one will lose out who loves the Lord.

O pen your ears, children, and listen to me;

P ut your trust in the Lord, so that your days are filled with goodness.

Q uiet your tongue; don't be tempted to speak evil.

R un from evil, and run after peace.

S urrounded by His presence, you are never far from His attention.

T he face of the Lord is against those evil-doers;

U nless they repent, they will disappear from history.

V ulnerable people are especially treasured by the Lord;

W hen they cry out, He heals their souls;

X rays reveal their spiritual skeleton's wholeness.

Y ou will be tripped up by your own wrongdoing;

Z eal for the Lord, however, will redeem you.

- Pick a letter for your day; pray through the promise of that letter in the acrostic.
- Psalm 34 is all about how the Lord hears those who come to Him humbly. Let humility clothe you today.

The Lord's goodness covers us from A to Z.

30. Songs Make Community – Psalm 145

Around the campfire, in sports stadiums, in rock concerts, at political rallies, in Christmas carol services, on long car journeys, in karaoke bars, in community choirs—we love singing together.

Chances are, most of us started singing enthusiastically in toddler groups, in preschool, or at home with our parents or grandparents. Chances are also good that most of us have lost that enthusiasm and don't think we can sing any longer. Singing is for the talented few.

Everyone can make a joyful noise, and everyone—no matter their circumstances, disabilities, or bad experiences—can improve their singing ability and confidence by singing in a supportive group.

Research shows that there are many health benefits to communal singing. It increases protective secretory immunoglobulin (important in protecting us from diseases), improves lung function and memory, reduces stress hormones, and improves our mental health.

In a TED Talk in Melbourne in December 2013, Tania de Jong explained that when we sing, the right side of our brain is activated—the side that controls imagination, creativity, and intuition. The brain is like a battery: the right side charges us up, and the left side uses the energy for logic, practical activities, and keeping us safe. We need to keep both sides in balance.

Our information society bombards the left side of our brain with so much to process and deal with, it often eclipses the right side. One way to re-energize the right side is to sing in groups. This releases significant levels of endorphins, enhances learning, and establishes new neural pathways. It helps in healing strokes, speech abnormalities, and depression. As we sing together, our hearts actually start beating together.

Singing together makes us feel more positive, and when we are more positive, we are more open to others. Group singing enhances the feeling of belonging and enables us to be more compassionate. It gives us a group identity, a feeling of being a part of something bigger than ourselves, of being needed, and of having a purpose.

Amazing things can happen when we sing together.

Great is the LORD and most worthy of praise; his greatness no one can fathom. One generation commends your works to another; they tell of your mighty acts. . . . They celebrate your abundant goodness and joyfully sing of your righteousness.

PSALM 145:3–4, 7

- Find an opportunity to sing together with others: Sunday morning worship, a community choir, a sing-along in your home, anything!
- Sing some more!

Singing raises our hearts to heaven.

31. The Long View – James 5:7-20

Be patient, then, brothers and sisters, until the Lord's coming. See how the farmer waits for the land to yield its valuable crop, patiently waiting for the autumn and spring rains. You too, be patient and stand firm, because the Lord's coming is near.

JAMES 5:7–8

Many of the previous studies have focused on how God accepts everyone into His kingdom. We have been reassured that there are no conditions, no entrance tests, and no required qualifications to belong. And we have been challenged to accept others on the same basis. Everyone can belong, and it's not up to me to determine who's in and who isn't.

However, easy as it is to start belonging, there is hard work involved in continuing. As we enjoy the benefits of belonging, we want to share them, nurture relationships, and see others respond to God's kingdom. Think of the farmer planting his seeds. It's not too difficult to throw some seeds on the ground. They may or may not germinate, and the farmer could just sit back and hope that he'll have something at harvest time. But successful farmers take a longer view. They don't just scatter seed. They plow first, they dig furrows, they fertilize, water, and weed. They may have to pick off pests, cover young plants to protect them from cold, introduce bees to help pollination, prune, or a myriad of other jobs, depending on the crop.

It's hard work, and it may take years before some crops produce anything—think of grape vines or fruit trees. There may be setbacks: bug infestations, drought, flood, or disease. But successful farmers persevere and continue to put the hard work in.

We need to put the hard work into our relationships. The writer of Proverbs said, "Sluggards do not plow in season; so at harvest time they look but find nothing" (20:4). We need to plow, nurture, feed, pluck out irritants, and care. Above all, care for each other! This is how we can reap the full benefits of belonging, and there is no higher purpose in our lives.

God bless you as you continue to explore belonging to His kingdom.

Using These Studies in a Small Group Setting

These studies are suitable for anyone who wants to explore "belonging" in the context of God's kingdom, whether alone or in a group setting. If you'd like to use them in a small discussion group, I have the following suggestions:

1. The studies are grouped into six sections. Group members should read the five studies of one section before the group meeting, perhaps in their individual daily quiet times. If you meet weekly, this book will last for six weeks, or for twelve weeks if you meet every other week.

2. Begin the group meeting by giving everyone the opportunity to catch up on each other's news.

3. Use the Opener at the beginning of the section you are studying to get the discussion going. The Opener is meant to be an icebreaker, giving everyone an equal chance to contribute, whether they are gregarious or shy. Ask participants to cut out their voting slip for the section and select an answer. Anonymity is essential to the Opener exercise! Collect the answers, tally the responses, and read out the total in each category. Ask if anyone wants to share their answer with the group or wants to comment on the question. People are often encouraged to share when they hear that others have answered in the same way they have. And you may get a completely different perspective on the question from that one person who answered differently!

4. Invite someone to read aloud the Bible passage for one of the studies in the section your group is discussing.

5. Use the discussion questions as you see fit. If you think of a more relevant question, ask it! And if the group focuses on just one of the questions, that's fine. Don't feel you need to go through all the questions.

6. Leave some time for people to share their experiences with the action points at the end of each study. Which actions were they able to complete? Which action was too difficult? Why? Which action would they like to continue working on?

7. If you are the "group leader," you may feel you should know all the answers. On the contrary, it's perfectly fine—even advantageous—to leave a question hanging. You may want to do some more study on your own, or seek a church leader's help, and follow up at the next group meeting. The discussion questions are meant to get people thinking, not to direct them to a prescribed answer.

8. Finish your time together by praying for each other; that's a good way to build a sense of community. You may find different ways of doing this to suit your group dynamics. Encourage each other, but don't push each other, to pray out loud.

9. Encourage group members to look out for each other during the week. Our small group meets for a social every two months, which is very popular. It's an opportunity to invite others along (non-attending partners, potential new members, or those not ready for a formal Bible study yet).

Notes:

A: Starting Out

1. The Invitation OPENER: Have you ever refused an invitation? Mark your answer on the voting slip. What was the invitation and why did you refuse? Where are you with God's invitation?

After the group shares any thoughts they have on the Opener question, read one of the passages together from this week's studies. Then discuss any or all of the following questions.

2. Living with God on His Holy Hill: Which failures in life are the hardest to come to terms with? What are the steps toward forgiving yourself?

3. Cornish Lighthouse Myths: Which areas of your life could do with a little more light at the moment?

4. Remain in the Vine: Is it sometimes difficult to feel like you belong because you are the only Christian in your work/neighborhood/family? How can we offer each other support?

5. Set Your Thermostat: Do you have a friend or family member who is struggling at the moment? How can you show God's steady love to them in a practical way this next week?

Which action points from this section were you able to complete? Which action was difficult? Why? Which action would you like to continue working on?

Use your discussion to guide you into a time of prayer for each other.

Notes:

B: Helping Each Other

6. The Zacchaeus Dilemma OPENER: Do you feel more on the inside, on the outside, or on the fence? Mark your answer on the voting slip.

After the group shares any thoughts they have on the Opener question, read one of the passages together from this week's studies. Then discuss any or all of the following questions.

7. Extravagant Wisdom: How has God shown His extravagance toward you recently?

8. Digging for the Kingdom: Has someone gotten alongside you at some point in your walk of faith? What did they do that was helpful to you?

9. Who Doesn't Belong?: Who can you show kindness to tomorrow who may not deserve it?

10. Practice Hospitality: Think of a creative way your group can share hospitality with others.

Which action points from this section were you able to complete? Which action was difficult? Why? Which action would you like to continue working on?

Use your discussion to guide you into a time of prayer for each other.

Notes:

C: Equality in Diversity

11. The Spirit Level OPENER: How did you sleep last night? Mark your answer on the voting slip. Are you worried about something? Can you encourage those who haven't slept so well lately?

After the group shares any thoughts they have on the Opener question, read one of the passages together from this week's studies. Then discuss any or all of the following questions.

12. Creative Differences: Which person will you commit to getting to know better in the next few weeks?

13. The Quilting Challenge: How did you choose to get involved in this group? What about other groups that you belong to? How have you benefited from the diversity in those groups?

14. Doodling or Scribbling?: Is there a point of dispute rattling around your faith community at the moment? How can you work to help people on both sides of the issue feel that they belong?

15. The Tango We Dance: How has your impression of someone (not necessarily in this small group) changed over time?

Which action points from this section were you able to complete? Which action was difficult? Why? Which action would you like to continue working on?

Use your discussion to guide you into a time of prayer for each other.

Notes:

D: Resolving Community Problems

16. When Should We Give up? OPENER: Have you ever found it difficult to get along with someone who had authority over you? Mark your answer on the voting slip.

After the group shares any thoughts they have on the Opener question, read one of the passages together from this week's studies. Then discuss any or all of the following questions.

17. Build a Strong Dam: What "spillways" or safe venting spaces have you created in your relationships? What works when tempers fray, and what doesn't work?

18. The Tea Strainer: Have you used the four steps toward reconciliation suggested in the study? What was the result?

19. Striving to Belong: How can you encourage open communication in a group you are a member of?

20. Dealing with Conflict: What is the current burning issue in society? How can you build relationships with people on both sides?

Which action points from this section were you able to complete? Which action was difficult? Why? Which action would you like to continue working on?

Use your discussion to guide you into a time of prayer for each other.

Notes:

E: The Community Already Around You

21. Building Together OPENER: Have you worked on a joint project recently? Mark your answer on the voting slip. What skill or talent did you bring to the project?

After the group shares any thoughts they have on the Opener question, read one of the passages together from this week's studies. Then discuss any or all of the following questions.

22. Communal Responsibility: Can you give an example of "helping your neighbor" and how it would benefit the wider community?

23. Triangulation: Have you ever misjudged someone based on your first impression of them? How can our relationship with God help us avoid this mistake in future?

24. The Closest Place to God: Be silent together for one or two minutes, and enjoy God's presence.

25. The Thin, Slippery Rope: What goals have you set for yourself? Do they lead to a greater sense of belonging, or do they undermine your relationship with others?

Which action points from this section were you able to complete? Which action was difficult? Why? Which action would you like to continue working on?

Use your discussion to guide you into a time of prayer for each other.

Notes:

F: Rejoicing Together

26. Being on the Winning Team OPENER: Can you recall a big sporting win, or loss, that you took part in, either as a player or as a fan? Mark your answer on the voting slip.

After the group shares any thoughts they have on the Opener question, read one of the passages together from this week's studies. Then discuss any or all of the following questions.

27. Dry Stone Walls: Delight in the variety of people in the group. What are the range of ages, faith and ethnic backgrounds, jobs, experiences, hobbies, and any other categories you can think of?

28. Praying Together: What are you praying for at the moment? Is it a prayer for escape, or a prayer for the resources to cope?

29. Acrostic: Which verse of Psalm 34 speaks to you most at the moment?

30. Songs Make Community: Sing a worshipful song together! If you struggle for musicians or lead singers in the group, play a song from an electronic device and sing along. You may want to make this a regular part of your group get-togethers.

Which action points from this section were you able to complete? Which action was difficult? Why? Which action would you like to continue working on?

Use your discussion to guide you into a time of prayer for each other.

Notes:

31. The Long View

Don't stop being a group just because you've finished these studies; decide how you will continue to meet together and encourage each other.

Opener Voting Slips

The following pages have the Opener Questions for each Group Study. Cut out the Voting Slip for your study, make your selection, and drop it in the hat. You can keep your answer anonymous, or reveal how you voted; it's up to you!

A: Starting Out

1. The Invitation OPENER: Have you ever refused an invitation? Choose your answer. What was it and why did you refuse? Where are you with God's invitation?

- ☐ Yes, couldn't go
- ☐ Yes, didn't want to go
- ☐ Not that I can remember

B: Helping Each Other

6. The Zacchaeus Dilemma OPENER: Do you feel more on the inside, on the outside, or on the fence? Choose your answer.

- ☐ On the inside
- ☐ On the outside
- ☐ On the fence

C: Equality in Diversity

11. The Spirit Level OPENER: How did you sleep last night? Choose one of the options. Are you worried about something? Can you encourage those who haven't slept so well lately?

- ☐ Not so well
- ☐ Not too badly
- ☐ Like a log

D: Resolving Community Problems

16. When Should We Give up? OPENER: Have you ever found it difficult to get along with someone who had authority over you? Choose your answer.

- ☐ Yes, now
- ☐ Yes, in the past
- ☐ Not really

E: The Community Already around You

21. Building Together OPENER: Have you worked on a joint project recently? Choose your answer. What skill or talent did you bring to the project?

- ☐ Yes, at work
- ☐ Yes, in church
- ☐ Yes, other
- ☐ Not really

F: Rejoicing Together

26. Being on the Winning Team OPENER: Can you recall a big sporting win, or loss, that you took part in, either as a player or as a fan? Choose your answer.

- ☐ Yes, a win
- ☐ Yes, a loss
- ☐ Not into sports

If you enjoyed this book:

Please leave a review! It helps others find the book, and gives me feedback for future books in the *Steps Toward* series. Go to www.amazon.com, search for *Steps Toward Belonging*, and click 'Write a Customer Review.'

If you'd like to contact me directly, please do so through my website, www.sandysalisbury.com, or email me at sjsalisbury@outlook.com, or contact me through FaceBook: Sandy Salisbury Author.

If you'd like to become part of the *Steps Toward* community and receive news about upcoming publications, you can sign up to the email list on my website, www.sandysalisbury.com.

Thank you!

The Author

Sandy Salisbury grew up in California and Oklahoma. She now lives in Exeter, UK, with her husband, Graeme, where she is an active member of Exwick Community Church, regularly leading worship and speaking. Her first book in this series, *Steps Toward Generosity*, was written jointly with her father, Ted W. Nickel. She also writes historical fiction and teaches English and Math to international students. She enjoys family time with her two adult sons and daughter-in-law, playing guitar, walking along the beautiful southwest English coast, and Scottish Country dancing.

End Notes

[i] Sandhya Rani Jha, *Transforming Communities: How People Like You Are Healing Their Neighborhoods,* (St. Louis, MO: Chalice Press, 2017).

[ii] Cathryn J. Pearce, *Cornish Wrecking, 1700-1860: Reality and Popular Myth,* (Woodbridge, UK: Boydell Press, 2010).

[iii] Moses Michira, "How to Construct a Safe Dam," *The Standard,* May 11, 2018, https://new.standardmedia.co.ke/article/2001279965/n-a.

[iv] BrainyQuote.com, "Ian Gillan Quotes," https://www.brainyquote.com/quotes/ian_gillan_1012137.

[v] James A. Michener, *Tales of the South Pacific,* (New York: The Curtis Publishing Company, 1947).

[vi] Rabbi Yoni Sherizen, "Justice and Communal Responsibility," My Jewish Learning, https://www.myjewishlearning.com/article/justice-and-communal-responsibility/.

[vii] Abd al-Rahman Azzam, "Social Responsibility in Islam," About Islam, December 2, 2018, https://aboutislam.net/shariah/hadith/this-hadith/social-responsibility-islam-part-14/.

[viii] For a layman's guide to String Theory, see Virginia Dippel's article published on Einstein Online, "Simplicity in Higher Dimensions," https://www.einstein-online.info/en/spotlight/extra_dimensions_simple/.

[ix] Jonathan Bagger, "Einstein's Dream of Unified Forces," Fermilab, last modified April 24, 2014, https://

www.fnal.gov/pub/science/questions/einsteins-dream-04.html.

[x] Miranda Sawyer, "Bill Nighy: 'It Takes Me a Long Time to Recover If I See Myself on Screen'," The Guardian, January 26, 2020, https://www.theguardian.com/global/2020/jan/26/bill-nighy-interview-emma-on-screen-anxiety-confidence-playlists-football-clothes.

[xi] Suzanne Wrack, "England's SheBelieves Cup Final Win Was 'Toughest Game' Says Williamson," The Guardian, March 6, 2019, https://www.theguardian.com/football/2019/mar/06/england-women-shebelieves-cup-final-win-japan-leah-williamson.

[xii] Ibid.